Richard Scott

FRANCHISE AGREEMENT

LEGAL AND CONCEPTUAL DETAILS, IMPLICATIONS, GUIDELINES, PROFIT AND LOSSES

4. Lift Brands, The Parent Company Of Snap Fitness
5. Burritobox
6. Pinot's Palette
7. Expedia Cruiseshipcenters
8. Mosquito Joe
9. HipPOPs
10. Happy And Healthy Products

SAMPLE OF CLAUSES FROM FRANCHISE AGREEMENT

GRANT OF FRANCHISE

1.1. Grant.

1.2. Number Of Locations.

PERFORMANCE STANDARDS

Initial Performance

Continuing Performance:

Minimum Performance:

TERRITORY

Your Territory:

Competition:

Business Outside The Territory:

ROYALTIES FEES

Royalties:

Royalty Payment Timetable:

FINDING SUPPORT WITH A FRANCHISE AGREEMENT

SMALL BUSINESS LAWS: INTERESTING POINTS

WHAT IS SMALL BUSINESS LAW?

PICKING THE RIGHT LEGAL ENTITY

INTERNAL REQUIREMENTS FOR SMALL BUSINESS TYPES

- Corporations:

INTRODUCTION

A franchise agreement is essential to safeguarding your brand if you are expanding your company through franchising. In essence, it outlines the acceptable and unacceptable uses of your trademark as well as the essential components of your business structure.

Each franchise concept requires a unique agreement. There isn't a format that works for everyone. Your company will be protected, the franchisor and franchisee will have assurance, and everyone will be at ease thanks to a custom, expertly prepared franchise agreement.

A professional franchise agreement should include:

- ✓ The mode of verification/identification of the franchisor and the franchisee
- ✓ The time frame of the franchise, and any of the renewal rights
- ✓ The fee structure
- ✓ How the business is to be promoted
- ✓ The operating requirements of the business (linking directly with the Operations Manual)
- ✓ Legal and regulatory compliance
- ✓ The franchisee’s right to sell the franchise
- ✓ What happens on the death or illness of the franchisee

- ✓ Termination for breach
- ✓ Franchisee obligations and restrictions after termination

There is a solid reason why franchise agreements are nearly always offered to potential franchisees as being "non-negotiable."

Franchisees should all be subject to the same contract provisions for the sake of fairness and uniformity. Additionally, a strong agreement is required so that a franchisor may monitor performance requirements and brand reputation.

Do you have a fruitful Business-to-Client (B2C) organization that serves cross-markets well?

Then, at that point franchising might be the following legitimate step towards development. However, the degree of trust you place in a franchisee is high, which implies you need an unshakable legitimate agreement to coordinate.

A franchise agreement will secure your organization's lawful rights. Ineffectively composed agreements don't fill their proposed needs.

Legal agreements known as franchise agreements are made between a franchisor and a franchisee. They by and large incorporate franchise disclosure archives (FDDs) administered by the Federal Trade Commissions' FTC Franchise Rule. A franchise agreement fuses the rights and commitments of the franchisor and franchisee to permit and sell an organization's protected innovation and permitting rights.

Instances of organizations that utilize franchise agreements include:

- Convenience stores
- Fast food and chain cafés
- Financial guides
- Health care suppliers
- Health clubs
- Real bequest organizations
- Retailers
- Travel organizations

On the off chance that you intend to permit your business to use a franchise, you should have a franchise agreement to operate legitimately and effectively. Something else, your franchise arrangements can bring about pitfalls that cause issues down the road for you later. Guarantee that you have a reasonable franchise arrangement for your circumstance and that you see how they work.

HOW FRANCHISE AGREEMENTS WORK

A franchisee fundamentally buys the option to operate an organization under the franchisor's setup framework, playbook, and brand. Franchises have a proven plan of action, and financial backers need to benefit from their profits, particularly those with past experience. The franchisor and franchisee should by and large concur on assumptions and rules.

Here's the way a typical arrangement of a franchise agreement works:

- Step 1. Meet with the potential franchisor

- Step 2. Build up the proposed domain rights for the franchisee's area

- Step 3. Set the base principles for execution and related punishments for missed objectives

- Step 4. Decide the amount you will acknowledge in return for your items or alternately administration's utilization

- Step 5. Make the promoting principles and licensed innovation rights by which the exchange is represented

- Step 6. Talk with diversifying legal advisors to assist you with interpreting your notes and discussions into a durable report
- Step 7. Revisit the franchisor to audit the agreements
- Step 8. Schedule a franchise signing party for the two players
- Step 9. Make duplicates for the franchisor and franchisee and disseminate them
- Step 10. Store your franchise agreement in a protected spot and ideally with your different reports

Getting a franchise agreement together is a genuinely clear cycle. Nonetheless, there are lawful and monetary issues that you should think about cautiously. The thought behind a franchise is to help you make a huge measure of cash and gain brand acknowledgment. Guarantee that your reports mirror the level at which you work.

TYPES OF FRANCHISE AGREEMENTS

At their center, a franchise agreement sets up how the franchisor and franchisee will work together. It likewise traces what obligations and duties should be maintained by the two sides. Nonetheless, specific franchise agreement types may turn out better for one circumstance over another.

There are seven kinds of franchise agreements, including:

1. Master franchise agreements
2. Product distribution franchise agreements
3. Job franchise agreements
4. Conversion franchise agreements
5. Investment franchise agreements
6. Business design franchise agreements
7. Area development agreements

For some circumstances, a master franchise agreement is adequate. Be that as it may, your requirements might be distinctive as per your industry, market, and geographic area.

KEY COMPONENTS OF A FRANCHISE AGREEMENT

Franchise agreements fundamentally contain similar components paying little mind to the kind you use. There might be basic contrasts, notwithstanding, in the event that you need an exceptionally particular arrangement. All things considered, you ought to consistently look for a customized alternative when drafting your agreements.

The critical components of a franchise agreement by and large include:

1. Territory rights
2. Minimum performance standards
3. Franchisors administrations prerequisites
4. Franchisee payments
5. Trademark use
6. Advertising standards
7. Exclusivity clause
8. Insurance prerequisites

Cautiously think about the components as referred to above. They will establish the vibe and foundation for the relationship you share with your franchisors. Guarantee that your franchise agreements contain the essential arrangements and components for exactness and fulfillment.

PARTIES ASSOCIATED WITH FRANCHISE AGREEMENT

The parties associated with a franchise agreement are the franchisor and franchisee. While there might be third parties included, for example, franchising legal advisors and insurance agencies, the center point of a franchise agreement applies the essential standards as vividly discussed in the subsequent sections.

FRANCHISOR

Franchisors are the substances or people who permit and sell their franchise rights to a franchisee. They sell the authorizing, marking, and protected innovation rights to them. The business that is selling their privileges is known as the franchise and can exist as a physical business or an online organization, or both.

WHO IS A FRANCHISOR?

A franchisor offers the option to open stores and sell items or administrations utilizing its image, skill, and protected innovation. It is the first or existing business that offers the option to utilize its name and thought. The entrepreneur who buys these rights is known as a franchisee and the branch business, itself, is known as a franchise. Turning into a franchisor is particularly reasonable for effectively fruitful organizations. At the very least, a franchisor should plan to spend on business advancement, a lead store, authoritative report planning, promoting, and bundling plans, and selecting and preparing franchisees. Franchises are directed by state and government laws that require a Franchise Disclosure Documents (FDD) and other administrative reports involving a lawyer's administrations. As a rule, a franchise agreement normally will not protect franchisees if their franchisor defaults on some loans.

HOW FRANCHISORS WORK

The franchisor organization by and large gets an initial start-up fee, a yearly expense, and a level of the branch's benefits. It might likewise charge for different administrations. Notable corporate franchisors include Hertz (HTZ), Marriott International (MAR), McDonald's (MCD), and Subway (privately held).

Turning into a franchisor is for the most part a decent business alternative, particularly for enormous, effectively fruitful organizations, however there are the two benefits and drawbacks.

A Chain Store is one of a progression of stores possessed by one organization; if Starbucks (NASDAQ: SBUX), for instance, were to franchise a portion of its stores, then, at that point those would be owned by outside investors—not by the first organization—and Starbucks would turn into a franchisor.

BENEFITS OF FRANCHISING

Development Openings

An organization regularly will utilize franchising as an approach to grow its worldwide presence since it empowers them as franchisors to profit with the nearby information on their franchisees.

The franchisor organization concedes the franchisee the duty of growing in a space or nation and awards them the option to sub-establishment. In return, the franchisee expects the monetary weight of building a unit and pays the franchisor eminences for admittance to now is the ideal time tried plan of action, market force, and brand name.

HOW FRANCHISOR ROYALTIES WORK

What Is a Royalty?

A royalty is a legitimately restricting payment made to an individual or organization for the continuous utilization of their resources, including protected works, establishments, and regular assets. An illustration of royalties would be payments gotten by artists when their unique tunes are played on the radio or TV, utilized in motion pictures, performed at shows, bars, and cafés, or burned-through by means of real time features. As a rule, royalties are income generators explicitly intended to remunerate the proprietors of tunes or property when they permit out their resources for another party's utilization. A royalty is a sum paid by an third party to a proprietor of an item or patent for the utilization of that item or patent. The terms of royalty payments are spread out in an authorizing agreement.

The royalty rate or the measure of the royalty is regularly a rate dependent on variables like the exclusivity of rights, innovation, and the accessible other options. Royalty agreements should profit both the licensor (the individual getting the royalty) and the licensee (the individual paying the sovereignty). Investments in royalties can provide steady revenue and are considered safer than conventional stocks.

Understanding royalties

Royalty payments regularly establish a level of the gross or net incomes acquired from the utilization of the property. Notwithstanding, they can be negotiated depending on the situation as per the desires of the two players associated with the exchange.

An inventor or unique proprietor may decide to offer their item to a third party in return for royalties from the future incomes the item may produce. For instance, PC producers pay Microsoft Enterprise royalties for the option to utilize its Windows operating system in the PCs they make.

UNDERSTANDING THIRD PARTIES IN ROYALTIES

Who Is A Third Party?

A third party is an individual or element that is associated with an exchange however, isn't one of the directors and, in this manner, has a lesser interest in the transaction. An illustration of a third party would be the escrow organization in a land transaction; the escrow party goes about as an unbiased specialist by gathering the records and cash that the purchaser and merchant trade while finishing the transaction.

A collection agency might be another illustration of an third party. In the event that a debt holder owes a lender an amount of cash and hasn't been making the booked payments, the loan boss is probably going to enlist a collection agency to guarantee that the borrower praises his arrangement. Third party's work for the benefit of at least one people associated with an exchange. On account of a land exchange, an escrow organization attempts to ensure all gatherings in the exchange. On account of third party debt collection, the third party sides with the moneylender to recuperate however much of the exceptional obligation as could reasonably be expected and is boosted in like manner. Third party is additionally used to allude to re-appropriating certain capacities to an external organization to guarantee productive help for customers.

How A Third Party Functions

A third party may likewise allude to an entity that an organization uses to moderate danger. For instance, little speculation firms face trouble entering the business when huge firms keep driving the competition. One explanation enormous firms develop all the more rapidly is that they put resources into middle and back-office infrastructure. To remain cutthroat, numerous more modest firms rethink those capacities as a strategy for acquiring a more prominent portion of the commercial center.

Little firms set aside time and cash by utilizing versatile foundation with variable expenses for exchange activities, information stockpiling, debacle recuperation, and framework coordination and upkeep. By re-appropriating middle and back-office solutions, little firms exploit technology and processes for more proficient undertaking finish, most extreme working effectiveness, diminished functional dangers, diminished dependence on manual cycles, and insignificant mistakes. Functional expenses are decreased, consistence is upgraded, and assessment and financial backer reporting improve.

ILLUSTRATION OF A THIRD PARTY

Real Estate Escrow Company

A land escrow organization goes about as a third party to hold deeds, reports, and finances engaged with finishing land exchanges. The organization stores the assets in a record for the benefit of the purchaser and the dealer. The escrow official follows the headings of the loan specialist, the purchaser, and the merchant in a productive way when taking care of the assets and documentation associated with the deal. For instance, the official covers approved bills and reacts to the directors' approved solicitations.

Albeit the escrow cycle follows a comparative example for all homebuyers, the subtleties contrast among properties and specific transactions. The official adheres to directions when handling the escrow and, after gathering every single composed prerequisite, conveys the archives and the assets to the suitable parties prior to shutting the escrow.

Collection Office

An organization may employ a collection office for getting the payment of organization obligation. Organization solicitations or introductory client contracts regularly state at which time a collection agency might be utilized for getting extraordinary payments. A few organizations can carry debt for quite a long time, while others anticipate payment inside 90 days. The timetable relies upon the market and the organization's relationship with the customer.

At the point when a business would pay more in court expenses than the amount of the actual debt, the business may use a collection office's services as opposed to documenting a claim. The office may pay the business 10%

or less for each outstanding invoice, or it might consent to a huge level of commission for recuperated obligations. The office merges the organization's obligation and goes to work recuperating the exceptional equilibriums.

Payment might be nonrenewable resource royalties, patent royalties, brand name royalties, franchises, copyrighted materials, book publishing royalties, music royalties, and art royalties. Notable style fashion designers can charge royalties to different organizations for the utilization of their names and plans.

Third parties pay creators, music specialists, and production experts for the utilization of their delivered, protected material. TV satellite organizations give royalty payments to air the most viewed stations cross country. In the oil and gas areas, organizations give royalties to landowners to consent to extract natural resources from the landowners' covered property.

Royalty agreements should profit both the licensor (the individual receiving the royalty) and the licensee (the individual paying the royalty). For the licensor, a royalty agreement to permit another organization to utilize its item can permit them access to another market. For the licensee, an agreement may give them access to items they couldn't get otherwise.

PATENT ROYALTIES

Licenses, Brand names, and Copyrights: The Fundamentals

Have a splendid new idea that you're certain will make you a fortune? There's a critical advance any designer or artist should take prior to taking it to advertise: securing it with a patent, brand name, or copyright from the public authority.

Each of the three gives a lawful safeguard against copycats attempting to make a buck off your idea. Be that as it may, every assignment applies to a particular sort of licensed innovation, so know the distinctions. A patent is a property right given by a government authority permitting the holder selective rights to the innovation for a specific timeframe. A brand name is a word, image, plan, or expression that indicates a particular item and separates it from comparative items. Copyrights protect "original works of authorship," like writings, art, architecture, and music.

What Is A Patent?

A patent protects a unique creation for a specific timeframe and is allowed by the US Patent and Trademark Office (USPTO). By conceding the option to create an item unafraid of rivalry for the term of the patent, a motivating incentive is provided for organizations or people to keep creating imaginative new items or services.

There are three kinds of patents: utility patents, plant patents, and design patents.

Utility Patent

A utility patent covers the formation of another or further developed item, cycle, or machine. Otherwise called a "patent for invention," it bars others or organizations from making, utilizing, or selling the creation without assent. Utility licenses are useful for as long as 20 years after the patent application is recorded, yet require the holder to pay consistently booked upkeep fees.

While a great many people partner licenses with machines and apparatuses, they can likewise apply to programming, business cycles, and substance plans, for example, in drug items.

Plant Patent

A plant patent secures another and remarkable plant's vital attributes from being duplicated, sold, or utilized by others. It is additionally useful for a very long time after the application is documented. The plant should be abiogenetically reproducible with propagation being hereditarily indistinguishable from the first and performed through strategies, for example, root cuttings, bulbs, division, or grafting and budding.

Design Patent

A plan patent, then again, applies to the one of a unique look of a manufactured item. Take, for instance, a vehicle with a particular hood of front lamp shape. These visual components are important for the vehicle's character and may add to its worth. Notwithstanding, without securing these segments with a patent, contenders might actually duplicate them without legitimate results.

From 2000 to 2020, there have been 399,055 patents given in the US.

Design patents given since May 2015 last for 15 years from the date the patent is granted and don't need maintenance charges. Patents issued before that last for 14 years.

What Is A Brand Name?

In contrast to licenses, a brand name ensures words and plan components that recognize the wellspring of an item. Brand names and corporate logos are essential models. An assistance mark is comparable, then again, actually it defends the supplier of administration rather than an unmistakable decent. The expression "brand name" is regularly utilized regarding the two assignments.

A few instances of brand name encroachment are genuinely clear. You'll presumably run into trouble on the off chance that you attempt to bottle a refreshment and call it Coca-Cola or even utilize the renowned wave from its logo since both have been ensured for quite a long time.

In any case, a brand name really goes somewhat further, denying any imprints that have a "probability of disarray" with a current one. Along these lines, a business can't utilize an image or brand name on the off chance that it seems to be comparable, sounds comparable, or has a comparable significance to one that is as of now on the books, at any rate if the items or administrations are connected. On the off chance that the brand name holder accepts there's an infringement of these rights, it might choose to sue.

What Is A Copyright?

Copyrights protect "original works of authorship," like writings, art, engineering, and music. However long the copyright is as a result, the copyright proprietor has the sole right to show, share, perform, or permit the material.

One prominent exemption is the "reasonable use" regulation, which permits some level of circulation of protected material for academic, instructive, or news-detailing purposes.

In fact, you don't need to petition for copyright to have the piece of work secured. It's viewed as yours once your thoughts are converted into an unmistakable structure, like a book, music, or published research. Notwithstanding, officially registering with the U.S. Copyright Office previously—or inside five years of—distributing your work makes it significantly simpler to set up that you were the first creator in the event that you at any point need to go to court.

The span of a copyright relies upon the year it was made, as the laws have changed throughout the long term. Since 1978, most organizations have been copyright-secured for a very long time after the creator's demise. After that time, singular works enter the public space and can be duplicated by anybody without consent.

When in doubt, the author holds responsibility for advantages, regardless of whether the material is distributed by another organization. There is a significant exemption for this standard, however.

Materials you make for your boss as an aspect of your responsibilities necessities, for instance, commitments to a digital broadcast the organization distributes, are normally thought of "works for hire." The business, not you, holds the copyright. In case there's an ill defined situation, you can attempt to haggle with the publisher over copyright possession prior to creating the piece; simply make certain to get it in writing.

The Bottom Line

The choice to seek after a patent, brand name, or copyright relies upon the kind of licensed innovation you're attempting to safeguard. Regardless of whether it's another item, logo, or innovative work, enlisting your thought with the fitting body can assist with guaranteeing you partake in the your rewards for so much hard work.

TYPES OF ROYALTIES

Royalty payments may cover a wide range of sorts of property. A portion of the more normal kinds of royalties are book royalties, performance royalties, patent royalties, franchise royalties, and mineral royalties.

Book royalties: They are paid to writers by distributers. Regularly, for each book that is sold, the writer will get an agreed sum.

Performance royalties: For this situation, the proprietor of protected music gets a sum at whatever point the music or tune is played by a radio broadcast, utilized in a film, or in any case utilized by an outsider. An artist may depend on a private performing rights association, like ASCAP or BMI, to gather the royalties for them.

Patent royalties: Innovators or creators patent their items. Then, at that point, assuming a third party needs to utilize that equivalent result of patent, they should go into a permitting arrangement that will expect them to pay sovereignties to the patent proprietor. Along these lines, the creator is made up for their licensed innovation.

Franchise royalties: A franchisee, an entrepreneur, will pay a royalty to the franchisor for the option to open a branch under the organization name. For instance, the expense to work a McDonald's franchise ranges from $1,008,000 to $2,214,080. This incorporates an underlying establishment charge of $45,000 that should be paid to the McDonald's Corporation.

Mineral royalties: Additionally called mineral rights, mineral royalties are paid by mineral extractors to land owners. The party that needs to remove the minerals will frequently pay the land owner a sum dependent on one or the other income or units, like barrels of oil or huge loads of coal.

LICENSING AGREEMENTS

The terms of royalty payments are spread out in an authorizing agreement. The authorizing agreement characterizes the cutoff points and limitations of the royalties, like its geographic restrictions, the term of the agreement, and the sort of items with specific royalty cuts. Permitting arrangements are extraordinarily directed if the asset proprietor is the public authority or then again if the licensing agreement is a private agreement.

WHAT IS A LICENSING AGREEMENT?

The term licensing agreement refers to a lawful, composed agreement between two parties wherein the property owner allows to another party to utilize their image, patent, or brand name. The agreement, which is set between the licensor (the property owner) and the licensee (the allowed party), contains subtleties on the sort of Licensing agreements, the terms of use, and how the licensor is to be redressed. Agreement types differ dependent on the thing is being authorized. Licensing agreements additionally ease any debates identified with deals, issues of value, and royalties. A Licensing agreement permits one party (the licensee) to utilize or potentially acquire income from the property of the proprietor (the licensor). Licensing agreements produce incomes, called royalties, acquired by an organization for permitting its protected or licensed material to be utilized by another organization. A few instances of things that might be authorized include songs, sports team logos, intellectual property, programming, and technology. Permitting arrangements permit parties to control property and enter new business sectors without going through the cash to do as such. Downsides of these agreements incorporate building up a relationship with some unacceptable organization and the chance of losing an organization's standing.

UNDERSTANDING LICENSING AGREEMENTS

Licensing agreements outline the terms under which one party may utilize property that is possessed by another party. While the properties being referred to can incorporate a heap of things, including land property and individual belongings, licensing agreements are regularly utilized for intellectual property, like patents and brand names, just as copyrights for written materials and visual art.

Licensing agreements are broadly utilized for the commercialization of new discoveries and technologies.

As well as detailing all parties included, Licensing agreements need to determine in granular detail how authorized gatherings may utilize properties, including the following parameters:

- The topographical districts inside which the property might be used.
- The time-frame parties are apportioned to utilize the property.
- The selectiveness or non-exclusivity of a given course of action.
- Scaling terms, with the end goal that new royalty charges will be incurred if the property is reused a specific number of times. For instance, a book publisher may enter an authorizing concurrence with another party to utilize a piece of artwork on the hardcover versions of a book, however not on the fronts of ensuing soft cover issuances. The publisher may likewise be limited from utilizing the creative picture in certain promoting efforts.

LICENSING REVENUES

Licensing incomes, known as royalties, are a critical wellspring of income for a few traded on publicly traded companies. For instance, a significant kind of revenue for the traded on a publicly traded company Dolby Laboratories is the licensing of its innovation to customer gadgets makers.

The terms of royalty payments are spread out in a licensing agreement. The licensing agreement characterizes the cutoff points and limitations of the royalties, like its geographic impediments, the term of the understanding, and the kind of items with specific royalty cuts. Licensing agreements are interestingly managed if the asset proprietor is the public authority or on the other hand if the Licensing agreement is a private agreement.

In most permit arrangements, sovereignty rates are characterized as a level of deals or an installment for every unit. The numerous elements that can influence sovereignty rates incorporate selectiveness of rights, accessible other options, chances included, market interest, and advancement levels of the items being referred to.

To precisely gauge sovereignty rates, the exchanges between the purchasing and selling parties should be eagerly executed. All in all: the arrangements should not be constrained. Moreover, all eminence exchanges should be led at a manageable distance, implying that the two players act autonomously, and have no earlier relationship with one other.

INSTANCES OF LICENSING AGREEMENTS

Licensing agreements are found in various businesses. An illustration of a licensing agreement is an agreement between the copyright holders of programming and another organization, permitting the last to utilize the PC programming for their every-day business tasks.

An illustration of a Licensing agreement in the eatery space would be the point at which a McDonald's franchisee has a licensing agreement with the McDonald's Corporation that allows them to utilize the organization's branding and advertising materials. Toy makers likewise regularly consent to permitting arrangements with film studios, giving them the legitimate power to deliver activity figures dependent on well-known similarities of film characters.

GOING INTO A LICENSING AGREEMENT

The haggling force of the two parties engaged with an Licensing agreement regularly relies upon the idea of the item. For instance, a film studio that licenses the resemblance of a well-known hero to an activity figure producer may have huge dealing power in this exchange, in light of the fact that the maker is probably going to benefit gigantically from such a plan. The film studio in this way has the influence to take its business somewhere else if the maker suffers from sudden anxiety.

Those going into a licensing agreement ought to consult a lawyer on the grounds that there are intricacies that might be difficult to get a handle on for those without a profound comprehension of licensed innovation law.

BENEFITS AND DRAWBACKS OF AUTHORIZING ARRANGEMENTS

As referenced above, authorizing arrangements are legitimate agreements that are composed between a licensor and a licensee. Ensuring there's one set up gives certain benefits to the two players yet there are likewise some key defeats, as well. We've illustrated a portion of the key advantages and disservices of these arrangements underneath.

Advantages

The terms, conditions, and limitations governing the use of the licensor's brand, patent, or trademark are spelled out in detail in licensing agreements. Both the licensor and the licensee are fully aware of what is expected and required of them. This covers the timing and amount of payments, any additional royalties that would be owed because of the connection, the type of contract and the period during which the licensee may use the asset, copyright concerns, and the contract's expiration date.

A contract is a great way to save time, money, and difficulties. For instance, if someone chooses to use a trademark without obtaining a license, they risk being sued by the owner of the rights, which could lead to court proceedings, legal fees, and wasted time.

Licensors have access to various marketplaces and can maintain a great deal of control over their content thanks to contracts. For instance, a licensor may decide how to advertise their property. Additionally, it enables them to access new markets via the licensee without having to open up shop there directly.

Disadvantages

The risk of drafting a contract with the incorrect party is one of the negatives of having a license agreement. In some instances, licensors may be so eager to enter a market that they neglect to conduct their due diligence. This implies that a licensor can be bound by a protracted agreement with a business whose values conflict with its own. The licensee must follow the same rule, especially if it assumes without performing any research that a new product or brand would succeed in a particular market.

Additionally, all parties run the danger of losing their reputations and/or brand power. For instance, if one business makes a marketing error or becomes involved in a controversy, it may also put the other party at danger. This implies that both the licensee and the licensor must run their operations efficiently.

The licensor faces more competition after signing a contract. Even while the licensee represents the licensor, it actually engages in direct rivalry with the partner. The licensee also suffers losses. Because the licensee may reduce its own research and development if it depends on someone else's product.

Pros

- The obligations of each party are outlined.
- Reduces hassles, costs, and time.
- Gives each person in the relationship additional power.
- Entering markets without expending a lot of money to do so.

Cons

- Being bound by an extended contract with the incorrect business.
- The potential loss of corporate reputation or brand strength.
- Heightened competition.
- Reducing the amount of research and development.

LICENSING AGREEMENT FAQS

What Is A Licensing Agreement Example?

License agreements are frequently entered into by entertainment businesses like Netflix. The owners of the rights to the content provide the online streaming service the ability to broadcast it alone or in collaboration with other businesses. For instance, a major television series' creator might sign a licensing agreement permitting Netflix to stream the show for a set period of time as one of its offerings. In return, Netflix would agree to pay the content owner royalties on the subscription fees it receives from users.

How Do Licensing Agreements Work?

Licensing agreements are formal written contracts between a licensee and a licensor. The contract details the sort of arrangement, the duration of the partnership, the amount and timing of payments and royalties, and the scope of licensing that is permitted. Additionally, licensing gives both parties the chance to have control over issues like exclusivity and marketing strategies. Essentially, the contract sets forth what is expected of both parties.

How Do I Create a Licensing Agreement?

A licensing agreement should ideally be drafted by a lawyer. You establish the right foundation for a relationship with the other person by seeking professional assistance. If you don't, you put yourself at danger of facing several monetary and legal obstacles.

How Much Is A Licensing Agreement?

It can cost several hundred to several thousand dollars to draft a license agreement. You will have to pay an hourly charge if you use a lawyer. Simple contracts may simply take a few hours; however more substantial agreements involving multiple parties require more information and changes.

The Bottom Line

You must ask the owner of the property—especially if it is intellectual property—to sign into a licensing arrangement with you if you wish to utilize it. To make sure that both your interests and the interests of the property owner are protected, you'll probably need to work through a lawyer. Your financial assets and business will be well taken care of and you are ensuring a good working relationship with the licensor by spending some money to have the agreement prepared.

ROYALTY RATES

The majority of license contracts define royalty rates as a percentage of sales or a payment per unit. The exclusivity of rights, alternatives that are available, risks involved, market demand, and the degree of innovation of the products in question are just a few of the numerous variables that might impact royalty rates.

The transactions between the buying and selling parties must be willingly carried out in order to provide an appropriate royalty rate estimate. To put it another way, no agreements may be compelled. All royalty transactions must also be carried out at arm's length, which requires that both parties act independently and have no prior connections.

UNDERSTANDING ROYALTY RATES

How Pandora and Spotify Pay Artists

Sometime in the past, in the beginning of Modern times, pirates ruled the digital waves and music-sweethearts found, to their pleasure, that anything could be downloaded for nothing. Sales of recorded music crashed. Each artist was playing the blues.

Those days are finished, however the way to a business model that works for Web organizations, music makers, and recording artists stays rough.

Two Computerized Players

Spotify and Pandora are two of the big names in Web music conveyance. Based on use numbers, music audience members will pay for a wide determination and promotion free listening. Subscriber services have all the earmarks of being liked over promotion upheld radio-style programming. Each service sets its own royalty payment rates and changes them often.

They used to be very unique. Pandora focused on free, promoter supported music with restricted customization. That made it, fundamentally, a radio service conveyed over the Web. Spotify was essentially top notch radio. It has a free assistance, as well however its motivation is to drive the audience towards a membership.

For reasons unknown, Web clients anticipate a serious level of choice and personalization and will pay for them. The Pandora crowd started to recoil while Spotify's kept on developing.

Pandora began playing catch-up in 2018 when it presented a premium $9.99 each month service and a $14.99 family service. That pricing matches Spotify's services. The change coincided with the organization's purchase by SiriusXM, the satellite radio company.

As of Q4 2020, Pandora had 6.3 million paid subscribers and Spotify had around 155 million.

Pandora additionally is playing catch-up in its music list. As of not long ago, it had somewhere close to one and 2,000,000 songs and presently flaunts a 40 million tune index compared with Spotify's 50 million.

Radio Royalties

Through the quick growth and expansion of the Internet music industry, discussions have erupted among specialists and the business over the apparent absence of legitimate pay. In 2014, platinum recording artist Taylor Swift pulled her music from Spotify's platform to bring issues to light of what she considered lacking artist remuneration. She was back on by 2017.

The music business creates a bit of its pay from royalties that are expected each time a tune is played out in the open. Public performance includes music played over the radio or through Internet providers.

Royalties are payments made to the lawful proprietor of a protected work, which could possibly be the artist who made it. Performance rights associations gather songwriting royalties from music clients and convey them to the lawful owners.

The associations that gather royalties from radio exhibitions include BMI, ASCAP, and SESAC.

BMI groups a radio presentation as a transmission that endures 60 seconds or more. Every performance is categorized as commercial, classical, or school radio.

- Commercial radio exhibitions include music normally played on FM broadcasts, with a potential for rewards dependent on popularity.

- Classical radio is related with conventional instrumental and vocal exhibitions and nets 32 pennies each moment.

- Performances played on stations related with colleges or universities are classified as school radio and pay more modest royalties than business stations.

Truly, streaming organizations have attempted to stretch the limits a piece. Back in 2015, Apple Music offered a three-month free preliminary of its service and quietly told their labels they were not going to pay any rights on their preliminary use, however it later withdrew after a public grievance from (you got it) Taylor Swift.

Digital Royalties

Music streaming services keep on multiplying, as exemplified by Pandora, iHeartRadio, Apple Music, and Spotify.

Streaming music represented 80% of music industry income, as indicated by the Recording Industry Association of America. Total incomes grew 11% to $11.1 billion out of 2019 compared to the previous year.

The expanded income share from streaming can be ascribed to the greater number of individuals signing on to subscription services as well as sales from downloads.

The organization SoundExchange operates a fee collector for the industry, charging performance royalties for recording artist and names at whatever point music is played through a digital platform. As an agent of the music business in the computerized space, SoundExchange likewise has negotiating control over royalty agreements.

Pandora

Pandora brings in its cash the same way radio broadcasts do, from promotion that is inserted into the playlist. Evaluations are that about half of its incomes are paid out in licensing fees.

Pandora's monthly active users (MAUs) were 58.9 million toward the finish of 2020, which was down from 63.5

million toward the finish of 2019. As of the finish of 2020, Pandora had added 133,000 new paid supporters of its Plus and Premium services, finishing the year with almost 6.3 million paid subscribers. Clients have the choice to utilize Pandora free of charge with limited advertisements or pay a premium for no promotions.

In 2020, Pandora had a per-play royalty rate, at 0.00133 cents per play, as per Advanced Music News. At that rate, the business site takes note of, an autonomous artist would require more than 1.1 million plays to acquire the U.S. monthly minimum wage of $1,472 as indicated by their computation.

Spotify

Spotify offers a free service with promoting and premium services. Since its inception in 2008, royalties have been Spotify's biggest cost, representing about $9 billion since its dispatch.

The organization once ranked as one of the industry's worst royalty payers, however it is consistently expanding its payments. Its per-play rate was somewhere in the range of 0.003 and 0.005 cents in 2020 for most artists, as indicated by Digital Music News.

The most exceedingly terrible paying platform historically has been YouTube. Its rate in 2020 purportedly was 0.00069 cents.

Spotify's monthly active users (MAUs) were 345 million toward the finish of 2020, which was down from 271 million toward the finish of 2019. Premium subscribers, (for example, paid) developed to 155 million of every 2020 from 124 million in Q4 2019.

Of course, artists have additionally seen unmistakable reductions in album sales projections because of the growth of streaming services like Pandora and Spotify.

As technology has advanced, the scene of the music business has changed from radio stations to mp3s, and presently to music streaming services. Organizations working in the advanced music space have seen huge year-over-year growth because of paid subscriptions and on-screen advertisements.

Despite the fact that artists, for example, Drake and Lil Wayne each gross a yearly pace of $3 million from Pandora alone, a few artists say the platform isn't fair.

As Pandora and Spotify proceed with their quick development and income development, we may see more artists take cues from Taylor Swift in kicking the current royalty model.

Quick Fact

According to UpCounsel, a cross-country legal services organization, the industries with the most elevated average royalty rates are software/programming (9.6%), energy and climate (8%), and medical care hardware and items (6.4%). The enterprises with the most minimal average royalty rates are automotive (3.3%), aviation (4%), and synthetics (4.3%).

Examples Of Royalties

A writer may get a portion of the returns from the sales of their book. An illustration of the royalty design could be that the author gets 15% on net sales of hardbacks and 7.5% on net sales of soft cover books.

An individual can pay to open an eatery franchise, McDonald's or Kentucky Fried Chicken, for instance. A franchisee of the McDonald's Corporation has a normal starting investment of one to 2,000,000 dollars, which incorporates an initial franchise fee of $45,000 paid to the McDonald's Corporation.

The satellite television services, for example, Direct television and cable TV services pay organizations and superstations a royalty fee to broadcast those stations on their platforms.

ROYALTIES FAQS

What Are Royalties In Business?

Royalties are intended to protect the intellectual property rights of an organization. An organization may file a patent on development so a third party must pay them a fee to utilize that patent. Protected innovation can be as copyrights, licenses, and brand names.

How Do Royalties Function?

Regularly, the parties involved will consent to an agreement or arrangement. The understanding will lay out the royalty fees and payment amounts. For instance, there might be a fixed charge, or the fee might be a variable level of gross sales.

Royalties for specific items (like a book) may be based on the quantity of units sold. Royalties for oil, gas, and mineral properties might be founded on one or the other income or on units, like barrels of oil or huge loads of coal. In some cases, recently created intellectual property, for instance, the royalty percentage might increase as the sales increase. A few royalties are paid for public licenses. Cable operators pay The Copyright Office for the right to retransmit television and radio stations.

What Are Royalties In Stocks?

It is feasible to put resources into royalties. Commonly, a financial investor may get a normal month-to-month or quarterly installment dependent on an organization's deals. These kinds of ventures are considered safer than conventional stocks since they are not reliant upon the financial exchange or loan costs. Additionally, royalty investments add variety to a portfolio. Like stock, royalties can be purchased and sold.

What Is A Royalty Agreement?

A royalty agreement is a lawful agreement between a licensor and a licensee. The agreement gives the licensee the right to utilize the licensor's intellectual property in return for royalty payments. The understanding will show the royalty rate, or the terms and amount of the payment to be made, by the user of the property to the proprietor of the property. The agreement will likewise state the parties in question, the rights granted, and the time of utilization.

What Are Royalty Interests?

Royalty interest applies to mineral rights agreements. A royalty interest entitles the mineral rights owner to get a part of the minerals delivered or a bit of the gross income from sold production.

What Is Gross Income?

Net income is the total amount of sales perceived for a reporting period, prior to any deductions. This figure shows the capacity of a business to sell labor and products, however not its capacity to generate a benefit. Deductions from net income include sales discounts and sales returns. At the point when these deductions are netted against gross income, the total sum is referred to as net income or net sales.

The investment community once in a while calculates the worth of a business as a multiple of its gross income, particularly in new enterprises or for new businesses where there are not many different measures to use as the reason for a valuation. Under these conditions, organization management may unduly focus on expanding gross income at a quick rate to build the organization’s valuation for funding purposes or to acquire a greater price in case of an offer of the business. An unreasonable focus on net income can have various adverse results, for example,

- Issuing new products that have not yet been altogether tried, so sales returns are unnecessarily high and the organization's long-term standing is harmed.

- Selling in any event, when there is practically no perceptible benefit, basically to build the income figure.

- Engaging in false bills and holding exchanges to recognize income on things that have not yet been delivered from the premises of the seller.

Therefore, it is better for financial investors to focus on different measurements than the measure of gross income, like net sales, net margin, contribution margin, or net profits.

The utilization of gross income as a measurement has to some degree greater legitimacy in a services organization, since there are no sales returns that may somehow make a considerable contrast between net deals and net deals. Net income is otherwise called net sales.

The Main Concern

Royalties are, essentially, a way for creators, innovators, intellectual property owners, or landowners to bring in cash from their resources. Royalties appear as agreements or licenses that lay out the terms by which a third party can utilize resources that have a place with another person. Intellectual property comes as copyrights, licenses, or brand names. Royalties can be procured on books, music, minerals, franchises, and numerous different resources. Some royalty agreements are for a set period, while different royalties are procured in ceaselessness.

Heightened Market Share

As well as expanding its geological reach, franchising is a decent way for an organization to build its market share while limiting capital expenditure (CapEx).

Franchises can be more productive than corporate-claimed chains, on the grounds that as entrepreneurs franchisees are motivated to expand their outlets' benefit and are liable for their own overhead, like the staff. Less overhead can make franchises more beneficial than organizations, in any event, when their outlets are less productive than they would be in case they were run as corporate retailers.

Versatility

Dependent upon a franchisor's requirements, assets, and production objectives, the organization can tweak its franchise agreement to focus on large-volume national development or low-volume local growth.

Extra Sources Of Income

A franchisor gets extra pay through continuous royalties paid by its franchisees. Royalties commonly include a startup fee, a month-to-month charge that includes a level of the franchisee's gross sales, and may contain different installments relying upon the franchise's understanding.

Royalties paid to franchisors vary by industry, area, organization size, and monetary strength. All things considered, royalties paid to franchisors for the most part fall in the scope of somewhere in the range of 4.6% and 12.5%.

DISADVANTAGES OF FRANCHISORS

Some may think—somewhat due to the precarious money cost—that franchisees accept more danger than franchisors. However, there are possible inconveniences for franchisors, as well.

Capital Investment

Building up an establishment requires an enormous investment of both time and cash. At any rate, a franchisor should plan to spend on business development, a lead store, legal record preparation, promoting, and packaging plans, and enrolling and training franchisees.

Franchise Failure

Indeed, even with careful reviewing with respect to the franchisor, a franchisee could end up being a helpless decision—flighty, hard to work with, or unequipped for maintaining a business for reasons unknown. Or then again the franchise could become unrewarding for different reasons. Indeed, even with a demonstrated strategy, there is no assurance that a franchise will succeed.

Less Control

At the beginning, franchisees will, obviously, consent to follow their franchisors' preparation, deportment, and other instructions. However, after the special night is finished, that probably won't be the truth. Franchisees are people with their own thoughts and personalities, so conflicts can generally happen: a franchisee could become obstinate or troublesome, or probably won't have the option to impact changes as effectively as the franchisor had trusted.

Exorbitant Legal And Regulatory Fees

If a franchisee won't collaborate, or ends up being a helpless decision in other ways, legal action might be necessary; this can be both costly just as harming to a franchisor's standing among other franchisees.

Also, franchises are directed by state and government laws that require a Franchise Disclosure Document (FDD) and other regulatory documents involving a lawyer's services.

ROLE OF A FRANCHISOR

The connection between a franchisee and franchisor is innately one of advisee and advisor.

The franchisor gives persistent direction and backing concerning general business systems, for example, employing and preparing staff, setting up shops, publicizing its items or services, sourcing its supply, etc.

The franchisor's advisory job isn't free, nonetheless; it is essential for the whole bundle that the franchisee buys. In any event, when the relationship is solidified, and the two have been cooperating effectively, the franchisor still goes about as a tutor. A franchisor's parental job is a continuous responsibility. Indeed, franchisors by and large police their establishments continually—though some more than others—to guarantee that they are keeping up with the parent organization's principles, item quality, and brand values.

DIFFERENT STORE TYPES AVAILABLE FOR FRANCHISEES

- Freestanding store: A café, either recently developed or a current construction that doesn't share any normal dividers to a third party

- Shopping focus retail facade: An eatery that shares a typical divider, or dividers, with outsiders

- Gas/convenient eateries: An eatery that is a sub-or-shared occupancy inside a gas/convenient climate

- Special distribution opportunity (SDO): Cart or Kiosk locations that are referred to as special distribution openings and might be situated inside another host establishment, like a stadium or another retail facility.

WHAT HAPPENS WHEN A FRANCHISOR FAILS?

When a franchisor files for bankruptcy, the court will quickly force a stay of all actions against the franchisor. All in all, franchisees aren't permitted to make a lawful action against the franchisor.

As a rule, a franchise agreement will not protect franchisees if their franchisor declares bankruptcy. Indeed, franchisees are generally required to pay royalties and keep operating in the midst of a franchisor's insolvency.

The accompanying steps in the process are determined by the type of bankruptcy the franchisor decides to file for.

In a chapter 7 Bankruptcy, the entirety of the franchisor's resources are liquidated to pay its creditors. Organizations normally go this course since it's flat leaving business. In the present circumstance, it's profoundly impossible that the franchisor will actually want to meet its franchise agreement commitments. Subsequently, it's likewise far-fetched that the franchisee will actually want to remain in business.

In a chapter 11 Bankruptcy, a franchisor revamps their debt commitments and keeps on working as a going concern. Under this kind of bankruptcy, the franchisor works with its loan bosses to make a redesign plan while proceeding to meet basically a portion of its franchise contract commitments. A revamping plan once in a while requires months or a long time to finish.

Regardless, a franchisor's liquidation will probably altogether affect its franchisees.

REAL-WORLD EXAMPLE

Dunkin' Brands Group (DNKN), which used to be called Dunkin' Donuts, started activities in 1954 and has been franchising since 1955.

With over 130 years of diversifying experience, Dunkin' is home to two of the world's most recognized franchises: Dunkin' and Baskin-Robbins. As per its latest check, Dunkin' flaunts roughly 12,870 areas in more than 45 nations.

As a franchisor, Dunkin' licenses stores and cafés that sell Dunkin' coffee, donuts, bagels, muffins, compatible bread shop items, sandwiches, and other food items and beverages viable with the franchisor's idea.

Most organizations that offer franchising opportunities present a-how-to information for prospective franchisees on their sites. For the most part, this is complete, voluminous, and regularly written in legal jargon or standard. In its franchisor job, Dunkin's content addresses its would-be franchisees plainly and justifiably, as the accompanying example shows.

TRAINING OVERVIEW

- Franchisees should consistently manage their network with something like two people, one of whom should be the franchisee or another partner, shareholder, or an assigned agent. Yet, both should effectively finish the necessary training program.

- It takes at least 20 days to finish the classroom/educational periods of the Dunkin' Core Initial Training program—excluding internet training, in-restaurant practice, or travel time; this is offered at least 25 times each year at Dunkin' Brands University in Braintree, Massachusetts.

- The classroom and in-restaurant time depend on 10-hour days. A portion of the franchisor's necessary classes are just offered on the web and are referred to as online training. These classes will require around 65 hours to finish.

OBLIGATIONS AND RESTRICTIONS

Franchisees should give nonstop best efforts to the developments, the management, and operation of their business. This implies giving adequate time and resources to guarantee full and complete consistence with their commitments to the franchisor, their clients, and to other people.

Franchisees may not conduct some other business or activity at the restaurant without the franchisor's earlier written endorsement. They may sell just items supported by the franchisor and they should make available for purchase the full menu endorsed by the franchisor.

Franchisees are not allowed to sell or distribute products or services by means of the Web or other electronic correspondences.

MONETARY HELP

Dunkin' commonly doesn't offer to finance. Be that as it may, now and again, it might, at its tact, offer willful financing to existing franchisees for explicit projects like the acquisition of particular equipment or accelerated development in determined business sectors.

The franchisor has facilitated certain third-party loaning arrangements that may give financing to qualified franchisees. The amount of financing and reimbursement period varies by program, conditions, and reliability of the candidate.

ESTIMATED INITIAL INVESTMENT

Dunkin' estimates that the cost to open one of its franchises—excluding land costs—is roughly $95,700 at the low end and $1,597,200 at the very good quality.

FRANCHISEE

Franchisees are the entities or people who buy establishment (franchise) rights from a franchisor. They are regularly enterprising entrepreneurs that have insight in the business. In case you are a franchisor, you ought to choose franchisees equipped for maintaining the guidelines and techniques you made.

10 ESTABLISHMENTS REVEAL WHAT THEY SEARCH FOR IN A FRANCHISEE

Need to be a franchisee? All things considered, it takes something beyond tracking down the right establishment for your necessities and way of life. The way toward turning into a franchisee is one that requires both the franchisee and the franchisor to feel like they have tracked down the ideal fit. There are, obviously, monetary prerequisites, yet most franchisors care about more than the figures in your ledger. Some need franchisees who are consistently energetic, while others value prudent individuals with business abilities. Some are looking for business visionaries who will be prepared to sign multi-unit bargains, while others need a franchisee who moves toward the business as a part-time job.

This is what 10 franchisors at the International Franchise Expo revealed to Entrepreneurs they searched for in a potential franchisee.

1. Philly Pretzel Factory

"Somebody who will follow a system. We need somebody who has the innovative soul, however, they need to understand that we have a proven model here."

– Daniel DiZio, President and fellow benefactor

2. Cinnabon

"Owning a small business with passion, energy, and a can-do attitude... To get along with coworkers at Cinnabon, you must like people."

– Mark Hong, director of franchise development

3. French Fry Heaven

"I'm a person who started a business, and it went well enough that people wanted to buy franchises. So, when I was searching for franchisees, I was like, I need to enlist franchisees like me... I screwed up."

"Now, we brought on another president... He was unable to mind less about franchisees being like him. He needs to know: Do you understand what you're getting into? Do you understand the work this will take? Do you understand it will be hard?"

– Scott Nelowet, founder and CEO

4. Lift Brands, The Parent Company Of Snap Fitness
"What I need is a fitness enthusiast, a coach, or someone with experience operating a gym. The financial aspect of it is underdog to me."

– Joey Aunan, franchise development director

5. Burritobox
"Without a doubt, someone who enjoys marketing... The lead to emotional with the customer is prioritized. That is what we don't have. The machine doesn't have that."

– Dennis Koci, CEO

6. Pinot's Palette
"We like individuals that are outgoing, bubbly. Characters with heart are our specialty." – Haley Connor, consumer marketing

7. Expedia Cruiseshipcenters
"People that would be group leaders. Our franchise partners... recruit, train, coach, and motive a commission-based outreach group. So, the bigger their group, the better coached and trained they are, the more effective they will be."

– Jeff Warkentin, franchise sales manager

8. Mosquito Joe

"Someone who is interested in that work-from-home atmosphere. It's a decent husband-wife, a family franchise."

– Julie Green, marketing assistant

9. HipPOPs

"We're searching for a somebody who is a go-getter... someone who is connected with their local area, somebody with a truly amazing hard working attitude. What we're not searching for is somebody searching for an easy money scheme."

– Anthony Fellows, founder

10. Happy And Healthy Products

" We need someone part-time because we need to grow it gradually. We need it to find a way into their way of life, rather than taking it over."

– Tabitha Locke, national sales director

SAMPLE OF CLAUSES FROM FRANCHISE AGREEMENT

GRANT OF FRANCHISE

1.1. Grant. We have the exclusive right to operate and to permit others to operate a tax return arrangement business using our Operating System. Subject to the agreements of this Arrangement, we award to you, subject to Sections 3.2 and 3.7-3.9 underneath, a license to utilize the Marks and our proprietary business techniques and software to operate an income tax preparation business identified by the Jackson Hewitt Stamps solely at endorsed areas in the Domain portrayed on Schedule A. Neither we nor an offshoot will operate or permit others to operate in the Region an income tax return preparation using the Marks and the Jackson Hewitt Tax Service proprietary and business methods, subject to sections 3.2 and 3.7-3.9 beneath.

1.2. Number Of Locations. You must open at least one office, either a Booth/Kiosk or a Standard Office, and such Processing Center(s) as indicated in the Manual, in the Region by the beginning of the first Tax Season after the Effective Date of this agreement. By the beginning of the subsequent Tax Season from that point, one of your workplaces must be a Standard Office. For each subsequent Tax Season, you must maintain a Standard Office. When you open a Kiosk, you may not cease operating the Booth for any Tax Season without our consent, which won't be irrationally withheld or delayed if the closure measures in the Manual are met, except if you can't lease space in the National Account or Affinity Location the Stand recently operated.

PERFORMANCE STANDARDS

Initial Performance: You must prepare at least 500 federal income tax returns in the Territory Domain in your second Tax Season. In the event that you don't get ready something like 500 government personal tax returns in your subsequent Tax Season, you must (I) submit to us a business improvement plan by June 1 following your subsequent Tax Season that we support, which endorsement won't be absurdly delayed or withheld, (ii) carry out the business improvement plan, and (iii) get ready at least 600 federal income tax returns in the Region in your third Tax Season. We may expect you to open a second Standard Office or Booth as a component of the business improvement plan. In the event that you don't fulfill these conditions, we may, in our attentiveness, end this Agreement for cause by written notification to you given after May 1 after your third Tax/Duty Season.

Continuing Performance: You must prepare at least 1,000 government income tax returns in the Territory in your fifth Tax Season and each Assessment Season after that. If you prepare in excess of 600 government income tax returns and less than 1,000 administrative personal tax returns in the fifth or any subsequent Tax Season, you must (I) submit to us a business improvement plan by June 1 after such Tax Season that we endorse, which endorsement won't be unreasonably delayed or withheld, (ii) execute the business improvement plan, and (iii) get ready at least 1,000 federal income tax returns in the Territory in your next Duty Season. On the off chance that you don't fulfill these conditions, we may, in our caution, end this Agreement for cause by written notification to you given between May 1 and September 1 after that Tax Season.

Minimum Performance: In the event that you plan less than 600 government income tax returns in the Region in any Tax Season starting with your fifth Duty Season, we may, in our caution, end this Agreement for cause by written notification to you given between May 1 and September 1 after that Tax Season.

For Small Market Territories, all tax return readiness numerical prerequisites set forth in paragraph 2.3 are reduced by 35%.

TERRITORY

Your Territory: The region inside which you may operate the Franchised Business is depicted on Time A to this Arrangement. You may not work the Franchised Business at any area outside the Region. You explicitly recognize and concur that we can work or allow a license to others to operate a franchised business at any area outside the Domain.

Competition: We won't operate the Franchised Business in your Territory except as given in this paragraph and in paragraphs 3.7-3.9 herein. We may use the name "Jackson Hewitt" and the Marks or other trade names and Stamps to distinguish the product in order to commercialize, distribute, or grant licenses to or sublicenses to others to sell and disseminate our proprietary software in the Domain.

Business Outside The Territory: You may not find your Franchised Business office or Preparing Center at any area outside the Region. You may play out the approved services in your Domain for clients who dwell outside the Territory, however you may not venture out external your Region to perform charge planning or different services approved by this Agreement.

ROYALTIES FEES

Royalties: During the term of this Agreement, you should pay us royalty fees equivalent to fifteen percent (15%) of your Gross Volume of Business.

Royalty Payment Timetable: The royalty fees are expected and payable as indicated by the accompanying timetable or on such other timetable specified in the Manual:

(a) Semi-Monthly Payments. From January 1 through April 15, you should pay royalties on the fifth and the twentieth of the month for the Gross Volume of Business generated during the previous half month. For the period from April 16 through April 30, you should pay royalties on the next May fifth.

(b) Monthly Payments. From May 1 through December 31, your royalty payment is due on the fifth of every month for the Gross Volume of Business generated during the earlier month.

FINDING SUPPORT WITH A FRANCHISE AGREEMENT

You don't need to feel overpowered by the possibility of drafting your franchise agreements. Getting help with a franchise agreement and understanding small business law is pretty much as clear as talk with a intellectual property legal advisor. It is usually more affordable to recruit a legal expert to employ a legitimate proficiency than you might think.

SMALL BUSINESS LAWS: INTERESTING POINTS

WHAT IS SMALL BUSINESS LAW?

Small business law can cover a wide scope of subjects and requirements. At the point when you start an small business, you need to understand the entirety of your legitimate commitments, from employment law and tax requirements to how to set up the right entity for your business.

PICKING THE RIGHT LEGAL ENTITY

A fruitful business begins with setting up a business entity. Entrepreneurs should choose what sort of legal entity their business ought to turn into. The kind of legal entity you pick has implications for everything from the taxes you require to pay to the sum you can be held liable for your business activities.

The most common business types include:

- C Corporations
- S Corporations
- Limited Liability Companies (LLCs)
- Partnerships
- Sole proprietorships

INTERNAL REQUIREMENTS FOR SMALL BUSINESS TYPES

In addition to local, state, and federal necessities, certain types of private companies should likewise meet internal procedures.

- **Corporations:** Corporations typically have the strictest requirements for internal procedure. For instance, corporations must:

  - Adopt and afterward keep up with bylaws
  - Hold introductory and afterward yearly director meetings just as shareholder meetings
  - Record minutes for these meetings
  - Issue investor stock
  - Record stock transfers

- **LLCs**: While internal requirements for LLCs are less strict than for corporations, LLCs for the most part need to:

  - Hold yearly meetings
  - Issue participation shares
  - Maintain updated working agreements
  - Record membership interest transfers

- **Other Business Structures**: Albeit other business structures don't have numerous internal prerequisites, most entrepreneurs report significant business choices.

Essential Kinds of Small Business Laws and Procedures

Entrepreneurs should know about various segments of the law.

EMPLOYMENT LAW

In the event that you employ anybody to work with you in your private venture, you should understand business law. These laws can change by state, so it's useful to talk with an employment legal adviser to guarantee that you're following important guidelines.

Laws and guidelines you'll have to follow when you recruit representatives to include:

- Anti-discrimination laws
- OSHA guidelines
- Payroll laws
- Tax withholding rules
- Unemployment protection/insurance
- Workers' compensation

You could end up with a lawsuit in the event that you overstep business laws and guidelines.

TAX LAW

In addition to withholding employee taxes, you should realize how to keep tax laws and guidelines for private ventures. You need to record charges with the IRS correctly as a small business owner. It's likewise crucial for know the answers to any inquiries regarding deals and VAT burdens just as when you need to document business income tax returns.

TRADEMARK LAW

One of the principal tasks to take on when you're beginning a business is concocting your organization's name. However you'll probably need to begin utilizing the name you settle on immediately, that can make issues. In the event that you accidentally pick a name, proverb, or logo that is like another organization, they can send you a cut it out letter (or even a lawsuit) in the event that they have effectively registered that data. You likewise need to ensure that your own data stays secured.

Take these steps to try not to run into issues with brand name law:

1. Check if your picked name is accessible by visiting your state's secretary of state site and looking for enlisted corporations.

2. If your name is available, document a "Doing Business As" form, or DBA, in your state or district.

CUSTOMER POLICIES AND PROTECTIONS

You should have lawfully restricting agreements strategy (terms and conditions) to which your clients agree to be bound. This is particularly significant in case you are providing some sort of service. The understanding should detail particulars for utilizing your services or products just as any client commitments.

Similarly, you should have an unmistakable protection strategy that determines the client data you do and don't share. Laws, for example, the GDPR in Europe and CCPA in California doubtlessly apply to your business, regardless of where you are based in the event that you cooperate with customers in those spots.

LICENSING, PERMIT, AND RECERTIFICATION PROCEDURES

You should familiarize yourself with all licensing and permit procedures for your business' specific field. Kinds of licenses and permits you may need depending t on your industry include:

- General business operation licenses
- Health office licenses
- Health and safety certificates
- Land use permits
- Occupational licenses
- Sales licenses for regulating items (like liquor, tobacco, or tires)
- Sales tax licenses
- State certificates with third-party boards (like nursing or plumbing)
- Zoning

Most localities and states publish different required licenses and allows online. You need to keep your business in consistence so federal, state, or local authorities don't close down your business. The records your business needs to remain legitimately agreeable differ dependent on industry and area. Renewal requirements for these documents likewise differ, so you should check with your nearby business licensing offices to remain refreshed.

Common federal agencies and offices small businesses may register with include:

- Alcohol and Tobacco Tax and Trade Bureau (TTB)
- Bureau of Alcohol, Tobacco, Firearms, and Explosives (ATF)
- Federal Aeronautics Administration
- Federal Communications Commission
- National Oceanic and Atmospheric Administration.
- U.S. Department of Agriculture (USDA)
- U.S. Fish and Wildlife Service

STATE AND FEDERAL FILING REQUIREMENTS

Small Businesses likewise need to stay aware of state and federal filing requirements to remain legitimately agreeable. A significant number of these are progressing processes.

State Requirements

Although yearly documenting prerequisites rely upon a given business structure and the state where you work together, there are a couple of normal necessities, including:

- Initial reports: A few states expect organizations to present an initial report and fee soon after the business' incorporation.

- Franchise tax: A few states charge franchise charges for LLCs or companies operating inside those areas.

- Annual reports or biennial statements: Most states will require one of these documents.

- Statement filing charges: You commonly need to pay a fee alongside the yearly report or biennial explanation.

- Articles of alteration/amendment: You should report any key business changes utilizing this archive, for example, changes to:

o Name

o Address

o Membership

o New shares

Federal Requirements

Many businesses won't have to stay aware of federal requirements as long as they settle federal taxes and comply with the Affordable Care Act, which requires organizations that employ at least 50 individuals to report providing health coverage to the IRS. However, you should meet all federal tax commitments, which include employer and income taxes. You should likewise keep your federal certificates, licenses, and permits up to date.

Moreover, some federal requirements don't need ongoing documentation. Small Businesses should stay in consistence with:

- Americans with Disabilities Act laws
- Copyright laws
- Marketing and publicizing laws
- Workplace health and safety laws
- Workplace poster laws

CONTRACTS WITH DIFFERENT PARTIES

Small Businesses regularly need to partner with a variety of individuals to perform required services. Working with a legal counselor who comprehends the complexities of these agreements can assist you with securing your business.

In the event that your business works with any external sellers, you need to utilize suitable and complete agreements. You ought to never go into any plan with an external party without first setting up a legally binding understanding. A few instances of when you need to utilize contracts include:

- Having occupants on premises you own
- Renting a property from another person
- Purchasing raw materials
- Using outside services

Essentially, you will need to secure proprietary data that belongs to your business by utilizing nondisclosure or non-rivalry agreements. This may apply to things like:

- Customer or client records
- Special recipes or formulas
- Former employees/partners setting up competing businesses

Regardless of what part of business law you need to understand, work with an accomplished legal counselor to guarantee your business stays in consistence to operate successfully.

Here are a couple of influential reasons concerning why you will need to get legitimate assistance with a franchise agreement:

Reason 1: Affordability

Franchising attorneys by and large work on a flat fee or quoted hourly rate. This system guarantees that franchisors can foresee their legal fees instead of pay a heavy retainer. Recruiting a lawyer is in every case certainly worth the investment because of the degree of security that they give.

Reason 2: A Commendable Venture

In case you are not kidding about franchising your organization, you need to have a legal agreement that mirrors these values. Experienced financial specialists can recognize a deficient or insufficient agreement a mile away. Boost your chances to attract aligned people by making the investment in an expert and polished franchise agreement.

Reason 3: Structure Key Connections

Have you at any point noticed that people only call a lawyer after an issue emerges? Now, at this point, it is too late or impossible to do anything about the issue or dispute. By recruiting a lawyer to draft your franchise agreements, you build up a relationship with a legal expert that comprehends your business and upon whom you can call whenever an inquiry emerges.

Reason 4: Protecting Your Rights

Your franchise attorney can likewise audit new and existing agreements as you draft and get them. Record managements and legal audits can become tedious exercises for busy company managers. You can designate these obligations to your legal team.

Reason 5: Negotiation Help

Negotiation isn't an activity that franchisees and franchisors approach regularly. While there is some knowledge of the interaction required, having an accomplished professional on your side can raise your outcomes. Think about acquiring a intellectual property or franchising legal counselor into your negotiation conversations.

WHAT IS CONTRACT NEGOTIATION?

Contract Negotiation includes at least two parties examining the terms of an agreement to come to an agreement before making it official. Contracts are an normal business transactions that give details concerning what each party is legitimately answerable for in the business relationship. You may have an employment contract, one for a land transaction, for a business acquisition or merger, or between a business and a consumer.

During the agreement negotiation process, all parties will evaluate their responsibilities, rewards they can anticipate from going into the contract, and any dangers they expect. The objective of contract negotiation is for all parties to feel alright with the details of the contract.

Steps To Plan For Contract Negotiation

Since each contract is unique, your process of getting ready for the negotiation cycle might be unique as well. These overall steps can help you feel more confident:

1. Understand the objective of the agreement. There is a hidden objective of each and every agreement. Regardless of whether that is to secure your intellectual property rights or to merge your organization with another, know why the agreement exists and what each party is expecting to get from the arrangement. The objective will drive the agreement terms and the negotiation process.

2. Prepare for questions and concerns. However much you ought to negotiate an agreement that you find favorable, it is also important to anticipate questions and worries that other parties may have. This will both earn you some trust in the business relationship, but additionally help the negotiation process go a little smoother and faster.

3. Look up relevant laws. Depending on your agreement terms or on the other hand in case you're doing business with somebody in another state, you may have to check federal and state laws, and possibly city guidelines. Getting comfortable with the laws that may

apply to your contract can help you with ensuring you have the situation under control.

4. Become acquainted with contract laws. Each state's contract laws differ as well. These laws clarify what can't be included for a contract, just as what one party might have the option to do if the other party breaks the understanding.

5. Assess hazards. You need to consider any likely liabilities for sure can occur in the partnership so you're prepared to account for them in the contract. Consider insurance, extra expenses if the unexpected occurs, and any administration guidelines that could throw things off course.

CONCLUSION

TIPS FOR CONTRACTS NEGOTIATION

Regardless of whether you're new to contract negotiation or have experienced your fair share, remember these tips for a tranquil process:

- **Be patient.** Each party, including yourself, has the right to take the time they need to thoroughly consider their contract advantages and address different partners about the understanding. Be patient with yourself as well as other people as you sort out precisely what the agreement terms ought to be. Negotiating can be an off-kilter and slow process, however take as much time as is needed and ensure that everybody is content with and comprehends the agreement details.

- **Begin with a term sheet.** A term sheet is certainly not a legally binding contract, however it can give you a decent beginning stage when building and later arranging your agreement. A term sheet goes over the wide terms and conditions of an agreement and can be utilized as a format for your contract later on. Assuming everybody can consent to what exactly is illustrated in the term sheet, then the contract negotiation process will most likely be less stressful.

- **Use an expert.** Contract legal advisors specialize in precisely what you're going through. They'll have the option to help you with drafting the agreement, getting through the negotiation process, and ensuring that the end contract protects everybody's rights and interests.

- **Keep an open line of correspondence.** Correspondence is significant in any business relationship, however particularly when there's destined to be an agreement set up. An arrangement depends on trust, so you'll need to guarantee that you keep on being open about any worries you may have. Try not to stop for a second to examine anything you disagree with or pose inquiries about terms you don't comprehend.

- **Keep the agreement objectives as a main priority.** It's simple for feelings to get included when you're chipping away at negotiating a contract, but make an effort not to fail to remember what your fundamental goal is. As much as you have goals for the contract, you ought to likewise realize what might make you leave an agreement. You shouldn't feel you need to sign an agreement on the off chance that it doesn't line up with your objectives.

NEGOTIATE CONTRACT STRATEGIES

In addition to the essential tips and steps to get ready for the negotiation process, there are likewise methodologies you might need to explore when you're in the middle of negotiations.

1. Negotiate the agreement in chunks. It's entirely expected to look at the contract as a whole and start negotiations from that point, yet when the agreement is long, it very well might be ideal to break it into parts. At the point when you do this, you'll come to multiple agreements, which can keep the two players inspired to proceed.

2. Separate individuals from the agreement. It's extraordinary in the event that you coexist with the other party engaged with your agreement, yet attempt to isolate your feelings for them from the current negotiation. At the point when you like the other people you're working with, you may consent to things in the agreement that you would truly prefer not to, all with an end goal to fulfill them. In any case, you shouldn't think twice about things that you are fervently against on the grounds that it will make them happy.

3. List out your needs. Your needs can guide the agreement negotiation process, so ensure those are examined first. You need to ensure you get all you require for the main items prior to continuing on to areas of the contract that are positively less significant. In the event that you know what your needs are, it'll likewise be

simpler to think twice about on the most un-significant pieces of the agreement.

4. Use the "good cop, bad cop" strategy. In the event that you have a colleague that you're working alongside, it very well might be ideal to have one of you serve as the person who poses the hard inquiries and sets the bigger expectations. It ought to be the person who feels most happy with being in this position so their methodology is certified yet solid.

5. Research the other party. The more you think about the other party, the more you can expect what their objectives are and address their interests before they bring them up. Individual details can likewise prompt a more shared climate as you talk about normal leisure activities or interests.

WHAT IS AN ENFORCEABLE CONTRACT?

An enforceable agreement is one that has been discussed by between all parties, negotiated effectively, and has been endorsed by everybody named in the agreement. When this occurs, all the contract terms become legally restricting and each party should satisfy their piece of the agreement. An enforceable contract is only the start of a commonly advantageous partnership with a firm establishment.

In view of how significant agreements are, negotiating them is comparably significant. Going through the negotiation process will guarantee that all parties are cheerful and that your business relationship can be loaded with trust and understanding.

Printed in Great Britain
by Amazon

38851806R00056